POSITIVELY POOH

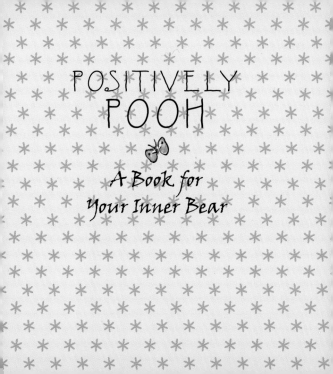

A Book for Your Inner Bear

EGMONT

We bring stories to life

First published in Great Britain 2005 by Egmont UK Limited
239 Kensington High Street, London W8 6SA

Selected text from *WINNIE-THE-POOH* and *THE HOUSE AT POOH CORNER* by A.A. Milne
© The Trustees of the Pooh Properties

Line drawings © E.H. Shepard, colouring © 1970, 1973 and 1974 E.H. Shepard and Egmont UK Ltd

Sketches from THE POOH SKETCHBOOK copyright © 1982 Lloyds TSB Bank PLC
Executors of the Estate of E.H. Shepard, and the E.H. Shepard Trust

This edition © 2006 The Trustees of the Pooh Properties

Book design and new text © 2006 Egmont UK Ltd

ISBN 978 1 4052 2048 1
ISBN 1 4052 2048 4

3 5 7 9 10 8 6 4 2

A CIP catalogue record for this title is available from the British Library

Printed and bound in Malaysia

POSITIVELY POOH

A Book for
Your Inner Bear

A. A. Milne
Illustrated by E. H. Shepard

EGMONT

Don't make excuses for your
increasing stoutness

'It all comes,' said Pooh crossly, 'of not
having front doors big enough.'
'It all comes,' said Rabbit sternly, 'of eating too
much. I thought at the time,' said Rabbit, 'only
I didn't like to say anything,' said Rabbit, 'that
one of us was eating too much,' said Rabbit,
'and I knew it wasn't *me*,' he said.

'How long does getting thin take?' asked Pooh
anxiously. 'About a week, I should think.'
'But I can't stay here for a week!'

Set realistic goals
for yourself

Become more flexible

He had made up a little hum that very morning,
as he was doing his Stoutness Exercises in front
of the glass: *Tra-la-la, tra-la-la*, as he stretched
up as high as he could go, and then *Tra-la-la,
tra-laoh, help! la*, as he tried to reach his toes.

By-and-by Pooh and Piglet came along.
Pooh was telling Piglet in a singing voice that
it didn't seem to matter, if he didn't get any fatter,
and he didn't *think* he was getting any fatter . . .

Being stout and healthy is better than slim and unfit

Read more
Sustaining Books

Bear began to sigh, and then found he
couldn't because he was so tightly stuck;
and a tear rolled down his eye, as he said:
'Then would you read a Sustaining Book,
such as would help and comfort a
Wedged Bear in Great Tightness?'
So for a week Christopher Robin read that
sort of book at the North end of Pooh,
and Rabbit hung his washing on the South
end . . . and in between Bear felt himself
getting slenderer and slenderer.

From little haycorns big things grow

'I'm planting a haycorn, Pooh, so that it can grow
up into an oak-tree, and have lots of haycorns
just outside the front door instead of having to
walk miles and miles, do you see, Pooh?'

Everything in moderation

Pooh always liked a little something at eleven
o'clock in the morning, and he was very glad to see
Rabbit getting out the plates and mugs; and when
Rabbit said, 'Honey or condensed milk with your
bread?' he was so excited that he said, 'Both,'
and then, so as not to seem greedy, he added,
'But don't bother about the bread, please.'

'Let's go and see *everybody*,' said Pooh. 'Because when you've been walking in the wind for miles, and you suddenly go into somebody's house, and he says, "Hallo, Pooh, you're just in time for a little smackerel of something," and you are, then it's what I call a Friendly Day.' Piglet thought that they ought to have a Reason for going to see everybody, like Looking for Small or Organizing an Expotition, if Pooh could think of something. Pooh could. 'We'll go because it's Thursday,' he said, 'and we'll go to wish everybody a Very Happy Thursday. Come on, Piglet.'

You don't need a Reason to
have a Friendly Day

We are all creative

[Pooh] had just come to the bridge; and not looking where he was going, he tripped over something, and the fir-cone jerked out of his paw into the river. 'Bother,' said Pooh, as it floated slowly under the bridge, and he went back to get another . . . 'That's funny,' said Pooh. 'I dropped it on the other side,' said Pooh, 'and it came out on this side! I wonder if it would do it again?' And he went back for some more fir-cones. It did. It kept on doing it . . . And that was the beginning of the game called Poohsticks, which Pooh invented, and which he and his friends used to play on the edge of the Forest. But they played with sticks instead of fir-cones, because they were easier to mark.

'I see now,' said Winnie-the-Pooh.
'I have been Foolish and Deluded,' said he,
'and I am a Bear of No Brain at All.'
'You're the Best Bear in All the World,' said
Christopher Robin soothingly.
'Am I?' said Pooh hopefully. And then he
brightened up suddenly.
'Anyhow,' he said, 'it is nearly Luncheon Time.'
So he went home for it.

Don't dwell on your mistakes

Concentrate on those things you're good at, not the impossible ones

'Well, we must be getting home,' said Kanga.
'Good-bye, Pooh.' And in three large jumps
she was gone.
Pooh looked after her as she went.
'I wish I could jump like that,' he thought.
'Some can and some can't. That's how it is.'

Celebrate others' talents, too

'It won't break,' whispered Pooh comfortingly, 'because you're a Small Animal, and I'll stand underneath, and if you save us all, it will be a Very Grand Thing to talk about afterwards, and perhaps I'll make up a Song, and people will say "It was so grand what Piglet did that a Respectful Pooh Song was made about it!"'

Keep your New Year's
Rissolutions

Rabbit.

wol

'The rissolution,' said Rabbit, 'is that we all
sign it, and take it to Christopher Robin.'
So it was signed by PooH, WOL,
PIGLET, EOR, RABBIT, KANGA,
BLOT, SMUDGE, and they all went off
to Christopher Robin's house with it.

'That's right,' said Eeyore. 'Sing. Umty-tiddly,
umpty-too. Here we go gathering Nuts and May.
Enjoy yourself.'
'I am,' said Pooh.
'Some can,' said Eeyore.

Do you remember the last time
you enjoyed yourself?

Modesty is the best policy

But Pooh's mind had gone back to the day
when he had saved Piglet from the flood,
and everybody had admired him so much;
and as that didn't often happen, he thought he
would like it to happen again. And suddenly,
just as it had come before, an idea came to him.
'Owl,' said Pooh. 'I have thought of something.'
'Astute and Helpful Bear,' said Owl.
Pooh looked proud at being called a stout and
helpful bear, and said modestly that he just
happened to think of it.

'Fourteen,' said Pooh. 'Come in. Fourteen.
Or was it fifteen? Bother. That's muddled me.'
'Hallo, Pooh,' said Rabbit.
'Hallo, Rabbit, Fourteen, wasn't it?'
'What was?'
'My pots of honey what I was counting.'
'Fourteen, that's right.'
'Are you sure?'
'No,' said Rabbit. 'Does it matter?'
'I just like to know,' said Pooh humbly. 'So as I can
say to myself: "I've got fourteen pots of honey left."
Or fifteen, as the case may be. It's sort of comforting.'

It is comforting to take stock
every once in a while

Don't try too hard,
let the hums get you

'Poetry and Hums aren't things which you
get, they're things which get *you*. And all
you can do is to go where they can find you.'

Balancing on three legs, he began to bring his fourth leg very cautiously up to his ear. 'I did this yesterday,' he explained, as he fell down for the third time. 'It's quite easy . . .'

Find a type of exercise
to suit you

Confront your fears together

'Look, Pooh!' said Piglet suddenly. 'There's
something in one of the Pine Trees.'
'So there is!' said Pooh, looking up wonderingly.
'There's an Animal.'
Piglet took Pooh's arm, in case Pooh was frightened.
'Is it One of the Fiercer Animals?' he said,
looking the other way.
Pooh nodded.
'It's a Jagular,' he said.

Make time for the things
you like doing best

fter they had walked a little way Christopher Robin said:

'What do you like doing best in the world, Pooh?'

'Well,' said Pooh, 'what I like best –' and then he had to stop and think. Because although Eating Honey *was* a very good thing to do, there was a moment just before you began to eat it which was better than when you were, but he didn't know what it was called. And then he thought that being with Christopher Robin was a very good thing to do, and having Piglet near was a very friendly thing to have; and so, when he had thought it all out, he said, 'What I like best in the whole world is Me and Piglet going to see You, and You saying "What about a little something?" and Me saying, "Well, I shouldn't mind a little something, should you, Piglet," and it being a hummy sort of day outside, and birds singing.'

You can have too much of a good thing

'It all comes, I suppose,' he decided, as he said
good-bye to the last branch, spun round three
times, and flew gracefully into a gorse-bush,
'it all comes of *liking* honey so much. Oh, help!'
He crawled out of the gorse-bush, brushed the
prickles from his nose, and began to think again.

Breakfast like Pooh to kick-start your day

One fine day Pooh had stumped up to the top of the Forest to see if his friend Christopher Robin was interested in Bears at all. At breakfast that morning (a simple meal of marmalade spread lightly over a honeycomb or two) he had suddenly thought of a new song. It began like this:

'*Sing Ho! for the life of a Bear.*'

He splashed to his door and looked out . . .
'This is Serious,' said Pooh. 'I must have an Escape.'
So he took his largest pot of honey and escaped
with it to a broad branch of his tree, well above
the water, and then he climbed down again and
escaped with another pot . . . and when the whole
Escape was finished, there was Pooh sitting on his
branch, dangling his legs, and there, beside him,
were ten pots of honey . . .
Two days later, there was Pooh, sitting on his
branch, dangling his legs, and there beside him,
were four pots of honey.
Three days later, there was Pooh, sitting on his
branch, dangling his legs, and there beside him,
was one pot of honey.
Four days later, there was Pooh . . .

Time to Escape for a while?

Because it's friendlier
with Two

So wherever I am, there's always Pooh,
There's always Pooh and Me.
'What would I do?' I said to Pooh,
'If it wasn't for you,' and Pooh said: 'True,
It isn't much fun for One, but Two
Can stick together,' says Pooh, says he.
'That's how it is,' says Pooh.

Take more meals together

Christopher Robin sat at
one end, and Pooh sat
at the other, and between
them on one side were
Owl and Eeyore and

Piglet, and between them on the other side were Rabbit, and Roo and Kanga. And all Rabbit's friends and relations spread themselves about on the grass, and waited hopefully in case anybody spoke to them, or dropped anything, or asked them the time.

Learn new things and be inspired

Suddenly Christopher Robin began to tell Pooh about some of the things: People called Kings and Queens and something called Factors, and a place called Europe, and an island in the middle of the sea where no ships came, and how you make a Suction Pump (if you want to), and when Knights were Knighted, and what comes from Brazil. And Pooh, his back against one of the sixty-something trees, and his paws folded in front of him, said 'Oh!' and 'I don't know,' and thought how wonderful it would be to have a Real Brain which could tell you things. And by-and-by Christopher Robin came to an end of the things, and was silent, and he sat there looking out over the world, and wishing it wouldn't stop.

Friendly walks are the very best kind

At first as they stumped along the path which edged
the Hundred Acre Wood, they didn't say much to
each other; but when they came to the stream, and
had helped each other across the stepping stones,
and were able to walk side by side again over the
heather, they began to talk in a friendly way about
this and that, and Piglet said, 'If you see what I mean,
Pooh,' and Pooh said, 'It's just what I think myself,
Piglet,' and Piglet said, 'But, on the other hand, Pooh,
we must remember,' and Pooh said, 'Quite true,
Piglet, although I had forgotten it for the moment.'

Find a Thoughtful Spot
of your own

Half-way between Pooh's house and Piglet's house
was a Thoughtful Spot where they met sometimes
when they had decided to go and see each other,
and as it was warm and out of the wind they would
sit down there for a little and wonder what they
would do now that they had seen each other.
One day when they had decided not to do anything,
Pooh made up a verse about it, so that everybody
should know what the place was for.

This warm and sunny Spot
Belongs to Pooh.
And here he wonders what
He's going to do.
Oh, bother, I forgot –
It's Piglet's too.

A friendly paw
will reassure

Piglet sidled up to Pooh from behind.
'Pooh!' he whispered.
'Yes, Piglet?'
'Nothing,' said Piglet, taking Pooh's paw.
'I just wanted to be sure of you.'

Leave behind the things that do not matter

Christopher Robin came down from the Forest to the bridge, feeling all sunny and careless, and just as if twice nineteen didn't matter a bit, as it didn't on such a happy afternoon, and he thought that if he stood on the bottom rail of the bridge, and leant over, and watched the river slipping slowly away beneath him, then he would suddenly know everything that there was to be known, and he would be able to tell Pooh, who wasn't quite sure about some of it.